WASHINGTON, D.C.

MALLARD
PRESS

Photography
FPG International
Odyssey Publishing Ltd.

Photo Editor
Annette Lerner

Photo Researcher
Leora Kahn

MALLARD PRESS

An imprint of BDD Promotional
Book Company Inc., 666 Fifth
Avenue, New York, NY 10103

Mallard Press and its
accompanying design and logo are
trademarks of BDD Promotional
Book Company, Inc.

Color separations by Advance
Laser Graphic Arts, Hong Kong.

Printed and bound by Leefung
Asco Ltd., Hong Kong.

ISBN 0-7924-5486-3

*Previous page: Lady Bird
Johnson Park, on the banks of
the Potomac River. Inscribed on
the walls of the Jefferson
Monument (right), beyond the
statue of Thomas Jefferson, are
the famous opening words of the
Declaration of Independence.*

It has often been compared to Paris and a large part of it was once known as Rome, but Washington, D.C., is different from nearly every other world capital because government is its only business.

Its creation was a classic example of government at work. Bickering among the states over which one of them should have the capital city was settled in a compromise: it would be in a federal district, not in a state. The new President, George Washington, favored a spot along the banks of the Potomac River, but representatives of the Northern states balked at the idea of relocating in the South. The arm-twisting that made them see things Washington's way was applied by Secretary of State Thomas Jefferson. Jefferson convinced Treasury Secretary Alexander Hamilton that he could transfer the Revolutionary War debts of the individual states to the federal government if he'd use his influence among the Northerners to vote for the President's suggestion.

The idea of getting out of the debts did the trick. However, when Congress voted to create a new city, it didn't appropriate much more than enough to build a Capitol for its members, a Palace for the President and a Navy Yard to protect them. But the planters who already had farms on the ten-square-mile-plot that had been designated as the District of Columbia expected to be paid for their land.

Among the landowners there was a farmer obviously impressed by the hills who named his plantation "Rome" and insisted on calling Goose Creek the River Tiber. But in spite of his pretentions, this farmer was offered the same $66 an acre for his land as neighbors were. The price was fair enough, but there was a catch – they were only to be paid for land that was used for buildings; any acreage that was to be used for thoroughfares and parks was expected to be donated.

When the landowners accepted the proposition, they hadn't accounted for the dream of Major Pierre Charles L'Enfant, the man hired to design the new Federal City. The Parisian native, a son of one of the gardeners at Versailles, had a very grand dream indeed. The planters were stunned when President Washington arrived at a Georgetown tavern with L'Enfant's plan under his arm. Of the 6,611 acres included in it, only 541 were earmarked for public buildings and a staggering 3,600 acres was to be taken up by streets and avenues. As the planters reached for another drink, Washington pulled an ace from his sleeve; add 541 to 3,600, he pointed out, and you account for only 4,141 acres, which left 2,470 acres unused. And that, he told them, could be sold as commercial property. Then, as visions of riches danced in their heads, the President took the wind out of their sails by pointing out that all of the land would be held in title by the federal government. But he promised them that, as the original owners, they would be entitled to half the proceeds of any of their former property that was sold for commercial uses.

Meanwhile, L'Enfant was bustling across the marshes marking off his 400-foot boulevards and 130-foot streets. He was adamantly opposed to commercializing any of it and cautioned that selling undeveloped land would bring low prices and encourage future speculation. When the time came to auction off the commercial lots, L'Enfant announced that his plan wasn't available. It was in Philadelphia, he said. Without a plan, the sale fell flat and when the auction was rescheduled, the engineer conveniently mislaid the plan again. Eleven months into the project, Major L'Enfant was fired. But for the next twenty years he walked the streets of the new city passing silent judgement on the way his plan had been altered, though gratified by how few changes were made. Most of the planters lived to enjoy nice profits on their land in spite of the tracts they were forced to give away to make the federal city open and inviting.

The District of Columbia had been created by compromise and artful politics. But the artist who refused to compromise won in the end, and though Washington, D.C., has grown in size and grown more beautiful since Pierre Charles L'Enfant dreamed his dream of a capital city worthy of a great nation, his personality is still very much alive in its streets and parks and the placement of its monuments. The city itself is his monument.

Like the city of Washington itself, the White House (facing page) was custom built. Designed by James Hoban, and echoing the style of Leinster House in his native Ireland, the original building was considered less than welcoming by its first inhabitants. President John Adams arrived to find a cold, incomplete, and unfurnished house, set amid the raw beginnings of the city. The residence's nickname is believed to come from the white paint used to cover its charred walls after it had been burned down by the British in 1814. It was not until the presidency of Theodore Roosevelt, however, that the name was officially recognized. The elegant proportions of the Capitol Building (above) and the National Gallery of Art (left) lend a Classical air to a modern city.

Although the idea of building a Roman Catholic shrine was born in the first decade of the twentieth century, the National Shrine of the Immaculate Conception (facing page) was only completed in 1959. Ingenious ways of raising money were devised to help pay for the shrine, including asking every Catholic woman in America named Mary to contribute one dollar. There was some doubt as to whether the project, which came to a complete standstill during the Depression, would ever be completed. The cathedral's tiled dome and distinctive blue and gold spire now constitute a popular city landmark. Right: a foreshortened view of the Mall at night encompasses the Lincoln Memorial, the Washington Monument, and the Capitol.

A fine example of a pre-Revolutionary plantation, Mount Vernon (right) the country home of George Washington, has been preserved as a national monument. George Washington wrote " ... I can truly say I had rather be at Mount Vernon with a friend or two about me, than to be attended at the Seat of Government by Officers of State and the Representatives of every Power in Europe." The estate is set in idyllic countryside on the banks of the Potomac River, and it is easy to see why it so captured the heart of America's first president. Below: a beautiful Georgian town house.

Felix W. de Weldon's bronze statue is based on an award-winning photograph by Joe Rosenthal, and stands just outside Arlington Cemetery. The sculpture, popularly known as the Iwo Jima Statue, *honors those men of the Marine Corps who died in the World War II battle for the Pacific Island of Iwo Jima.*

Ordered rows of graves surround
the white marble Memorial
Amphitheater in Arlington
National Cemetery (right). In the
Amphitheater's Plaza stands the
Tomb of the Unknown Soldier.
Built to commemorate the
unknown dead of World War I,
World War II, and the Korean
War, the Tomb is guarded around
the clock. The Vietnam Veterans
Memorial (above right), a simple
V-shaped wall, honors those
killed in the Vietnam War.
Engraved in chronological order
on its polished, marble surface
are the names of every American
who died and those who are still
missing. The Three Servicemen
(above), depicts the youthfulness
of those who fought in Vietnam.
and stands alongside the
Veterans Memorial in Constitution
Gardens.

The facade of the Library of
Congress (facing page) is
reminiscent of the Paris Opera
House. Researchers in the
Library's ornate, octagonal
Reading Room (below) are
surrounded by statues of the
world's greatest philosophers.
The Library's growth was
guaranteed by copyright 'law that
ensured the Library received two
copies of any book before
copyright could be granted. Now
the largest and one of the most
diverse collections in the world, it
is open to anyone over the age of
eighteen. Right: the Declaration
of Independence, the Constitution
and the Bill of Rights on display in
the National Archives.

Work on the Capitol's magnificent dome (these pages) continued throughout the Civil War, even though the building had been turned into a temporary hospital. The General Ulysses S. Grant Memorial (facing page), at the base of the Capitol lawn, depicts the full horror of the War.

An aerial photograph of Washington, D.C. (facing page) shows how the major axes of the city are centered on the Rotunda of the Capitol, just as the city's designer, L'Enfant, originally intended. The centerpiece of the Rotunda's symbolically-decorated interior (right) is Brumidi's, *Apotheosis of George Washington. In order to appear life-size to onlookers 180 feet below, the figures had to be painted over fifteen feet tall. As dawn rises, soft shadows from the Jefferson Memorial (below) are cast into the Tidal Basin.*

Only one side of the famous five-sided Pentagon is visible from the Columbia Marina (facing page). Staffed by both military and civilian personnel, the Pentagon is the stronghold of the Department of Defense, and the world's largest office building. Housing only a fraction of the Treasury Department's staff, the Treasury Building (above) was built to the east of the White House, blocking the view of the Capitol intended by L'Enfant. Some have light-heartedly maintained that this was done deliberately by Andrew Jackson in an effort to forget his problems with Congress. Right: a reproduction of the Liberty Bell on the steps of the Treasury Building.

English scientist James Smithson, founder of the Smithsonian Institution, cannot have envisaged the size to which the collection would grow. Smithson, whose goal was the "increase and diffusion of knowledge among men," made a bequest of half a million dollars, his entire fortune, that formed the financial basis from which the Institution grew. At one time housing the entire collection, the red sandstone "Castle" (left) is now used solely for administration. Visitors to the National Museum of Natural History (below), part of the Smithsonian, are greeted by a thirteen-foot-tall African bush elephant.

Since its creation in 1976, the Smithsonian's National Air and Space Museum has proved one of Washington's most popular museums. Through an exciting collection of exhibits, the mysteries of flight, particularly space flight, are explained to a fascinated public.

Exhibited on the layered terraces of the Hirshhorn Museum's Sculpture Garden (facing page) are works by contemporary American and European sculptors, some of which have been acquired since the bulk of the collection was donated to the nation by the financier Joseph Hirshhorn. Right: the East Building of the National Gallery of Art.

A fountain (above), with the graceful figure of Mercury poised on top, rises from the floor of the rotunda of the National Gallery of Art. Lined with quiet alcoves, the rotunda is the point from which the building's two wings stretch out. The National Gallery's growing collection, spanning medieval times to the present day, is now partly accommodated in the modern East Building. Measuring thirty-four feet in circumference, the massive freestanding globe (right) in the Explorers Hall of the National Geographic Society is perhaps the latter's most well-known symbol. Established in 1888 with the aim of furthering geographical knowledge, the Society has helped to fund both research projects and expeditions. Memorabilia from these projects, including Jacques Cousteau's diving saucer and the dog sleds used by Robert Peary in his 1909 expedition to the North Pole, are on display in the museum.

The statue of General Andrew Jackson (above) stands outside the White House. The J. Edgar Hoover Building (right), headquarters of the Federal Bureau of Investigation, is a monument of a different kind. Director of the Bureau from 1924 until his death in 1972, Hoover was responsible for its reorganization. Though many have disagreed with the methods he employed, his considerable achievement in turning a once disreputable department into one which is renowned the world over cannot be denied. The Church of Jesus Christ of Latter-Day Saints (facing page), situated in Kensington, Maryland, is the only Mormon temple east of the Mississippi River.

At night the white marble walls of the Lincoln Memorial are illuminated. Between the dark pillars sits a statue Lincoln himself, gazing broodily over the city.

The sharply defined lines of the Washington Monument (left) shimmer in the Reflecting Pool. On the steps of the Capitol, the site of most Presidential inaugurations since Andrew Jackson, people linger to listen to the music of a band (right).

The stone tablet and sword held by the figures at the entrance to the U.S. Supreme Court Building (facing page) represent the law and its enforcement respectively. As the highest court in the land, the Supreme Court has often been called the court of the last resort. The low arches of Arlington Memorial Bridge (above) support a highway that carries traffic from the center of Washington to Arlington National Cemetery. Plans for the bridge only received proper consideration in 1921, seventy years after they were first put forward, when the procession to the Cemetery for the interment of the Unknown Soldier caused massive traffic jams. Right: visitors to the Mall get their bearings at an information board outside the National Museum of Natural History.

Built in the fourteenth-century
Gothic style, the Cathedral
Church of St. Peter and St. Paul
(facing page), begun in 1907,
stands in shady, well-established
gardens planted with traditional
boxwood hedges and flourishing
rose bushes. Part of the
cathedral's charm lies in the
startling colors of its modern
stained glass windows (right).
The windows, beautiful in
themselves, also cast
multicolored trails of light onto the
limestone walls as the sun's rays
pass through them. Dwarfed by
the Classical columns, tourists
climbing the steps of the Lincoln
Memorial (below), bring its sheer
scale into perspective.

An everyday, working Washington exists behind the monuments and the museums. This, like any other modern city, is served by a sophisticated transport system. The graffiti-proof terrazzo tiles and fluorescent floor lighting of the Washington Metro (above) are only part of the five-star service that it offers. Clean, modern, and efficient, the Washington Metro epitomizes the city's working spirit. Practicality and architectural innovation are brought together in Dulles International Airport (facing page). The airport, completed in 1962, was the first to be designed specifically for jet aircraft.

Piercing the sky, the Washington Monument (facing page) rises 550 feet into the air. In the style of a traditional Greek obelisk, the Monument commemorates the nation's first president and one of its greatest leaders. Spring in Washington, when the city is awash with blossom, is famed for its beauty. The flower beds outside the National Museum of American History (below) and the Bureau of Engraving and Printing (right) are a mass of red and yellow bulbs. Overleaf: the Jefferson Memorial.